Albion Album

Robert Grieves

CLYDE BUILT. A specially posed Albion publicity photograph of 1932 taken at Queen's Dock in Glasgow. In the foreground are two new Albion lorries of the period. To the left is a normal control (or bonnet type) where the driver sat behind the engine, as in a private car. Registered in Lanarkshire, VD 1473 was one of the popular model 463 Albions in the fleet of Airdrie haulage contractor David Smith. The other was of forward control (or overtype), where the driver sat alongside the engine in the cab, in the ownership of the London & North Eastern Railway. Also Clyde built, like the Albions, was the 16,000 ton liner 'Transylvania', constructed at Fairfield's Govan yard and owned by the Anchor Line, sailing on trans-Atlantic crossings to New York.

Introduction

December 1999 marks the 100th birthday of Scotland's best known name in the motor industry (in fact for many years the only one) – Albion Motors of Scotstoun, Glasgow. The company was formed through the partnership of Thomas Murray and Norman Fulton both of whom had previously been involved with George Johnston's Mo Car Syndicate, which later became the Arrol Johnston Company. Albion went from strength to strength over the years and in 1951 Lancashire-based Leyland Motors acquired the company as the first step in a major expansionist policy which later saw Scammell, A.E.C. and Guy succumb, among others, in 1955, 1962 and 1968 respectively. The Scotstoun works was still used for truck and bus manufacture until 1972 when the last complete vehicle was built there, components only being produced from then. But perhaps the greatest indignity of all was the change of name to Leyland (Glasgow) and later to Leyland-DAF from 1987 when it became a subsidiary of that Dutch concern. Eventually in 1993 a management buy-out from that troubled company brought Albion Automotive as it was thenceforth known back into Scottish ownership. The latest chapter in the Albion story unfolded as recently as 1998 when the American Axle & Manufacturing Company of Detroit, Michigan, acquired the business. The traditional Albion name will be retained, however, and as AAM is a major force in the components market, producing axles and other accessories for markets at home and overseas, the future looks bright for another hundred years.

So many folk have been employed 'at the Albion' over the century that there must be few, especially in the Glasgow area, to whom the name is not familiar. As a small boy in the 1940s and '50s I always stopped to watch any passing Albion. To my mind there was no rival to the splendid sunrise radiator, which even to that boy spoke of solid and superior workmanship. Other makes were second rate in comparison. Albions which I saw most often were usually lorries in the fleets of the local Paisley haulage contractors William Cummings and J. & M. Taylor or double deck ' Venturer' buses in the colourful orange livery of Young's Bus Service which operated between Glasgow, Paisley, Johnstone and Largs. Whenever I was fortunate enough to have been taken by my parents to this Clyde Coast resort, it was an added bonus even greater than a Nardini's ice cream to return home in a Y.B.S. Albion, especially if I'd been lucky in gaining a front downstairs seat from where I could personally 'drive' the bus home by means of steering the big circular 'Clayton' heater on the front bulkhead. Memories, memories . . . but they are what this little book is all about. It is not intended that it should be a technical volume. 'Albion Album' is for those who can perhaps remember former days as an employee at Scotstoun or possibly, like myself, simply have happy recollections of those Scottish workhorses from the company whose famous motto was 'Sure as the Sunrise'.

I hope that the photographs I have chosen will evoke memories which recall those days when the famous radiator was seen not only around Scotland and the British Isles but in fact all over the world. Admittedly to many observers the image of Albion trucks and buses was rightly or wrongly an old fashioned one but I am not alone in believing that this formed the basis for much of their appeal. Their appearance changed so little over the years and most admirers of the marque would probably agree that this was perhaps part of their stamp of rugged reliability and the very reason that so many people still fondly remember yesterday's Albions today.

The illustrations cover only a selection of the many models produced over the years, not all of which are represented but here's hoping you find your favourite.

Paisley 1999   *Robert Grieves*

FRONT COVER.
The Albion 'Clydesdale' – a Scottish workhorse.
The 'Clydesdale' model was first introduced in the late 1940s, and was built in various forms of both goods and occasional passenger models right through until production of chassis ceased at Scotstoun in 1972 when the Albion name changed to Leyland (Glasgow). The 'Clydesdale' name continued to be used, however, into the 1980s at the Bathgate plant albeit for several different passenger and goods versions.
Artist Alan Spillet's impression of a 1956 'Clydesdale' shows AXS 146 working for Paisley haulage contractor J. & M. Taylor, traditionally an Albion Motors customer. It is seen near Barfillan in the pleasant Renfrewshire countryside between Bridge of Weir and Houston loaded with sacks of grain for delivery to local farms.

It is appropriate that an Albion 'Venturer' in the once-familiar livery of erstwhile Glasgow Corporation Transport should grace the cover. The municipality naturally supported local industry and accordingly G.C.T. was the largest fleet operator of the 'Venturer'. The bus seen here was originally delivered in 1940 in a batch of 30 with bodywork divided between Pickering of Wishaw and Metro-Cammell of Birmingham (who more recently built the underground 'clockwork orange' railway carriages for Glasgow's subway). Some were to have a new lease of life as in 1951 the Pickering examples, along with another batch of CX 19s from 1939, were rebodied by East Lancs. Coachbuilders of Blackburn, at their other factory in Bridlington, Yorkshire. DGB 468 was originally 820 in the Glasgow fleet, renumbered BR 27 with its new body and remained in service untill 1960, thus would still have been in service on the streets of Glasgow around the same period as Taylor's 'Clydesdale' lorry. It is seen here at Anniesland Cross where the tramway rails and overhead wires are also visible.

First published 1999

ISBN 0 946265 29 1

© Robert Grieves

Typeset and printed by
Cordfall Ltd, Glasgow

Published by
Arthur Southern Ltd.
5 Hallcroft Close, Ratho,
Newbridge, Midlothian, EH 28 8SD

THE ALBION CAR.

RELIABILITY

Thoroughly Demonstrated

in Glasgow

MOTOR TRIALS.

BRITISH BUILT

7 Brake Horse-Power

PETROL MOTOR.

THE ALBION MOTOR=CAR COMPANY,

169 FINNIESTON STREET, GLASGOW.

One of the earliest Albion advertisements, which appeared in the trade press in 1901. It shows a rear entrance model A2 tonneau with tiller steering and quotes reliability in the Glasgow motor trials which had taken place that year at Kelvingrove during the International Exhibition held there. Albion cars were produced until 1913 from which time the company concentrated solely on their increasingly popular range of commercial vehicles.

The first premises of the Albion Motor Car Company as it was originally known were in Glasgow's Finnieston Street from the inception of the company in December 1899 until a move was made to a new purpose built factory in South Street, Scotstoun in the summer of 1903. This scene in 1902 outside the Finnieston works shows a 10 h.p. rear entrance model A2 tonneau but with a conventional steering wheel by this year.

3

NS 21 was one of several similar model A 3 16 h.p. open wagonettes in service during Edwardian times with the Sutherland Motor Traffic Company Ltd. which was based in Lairg where this view was taken beside Loch Shin in 1905. This company, owned by hotelier Wm. Wallace who was proprietor of The Sutherland Arms, Lairg and the Inchnadamph Hotel, Loch Assynt operated combined passenger services and Royal Mail contracts to Lochinver, Durness and Scourie, later named the Sutherland Transport & Trading Co. Nowadays this sparsely populated area is served by modern post buses.

An example of a later Albion car; the 24/30 h.p. model. This type found popularity with upper class families who could afford to employ a chauffeur. SN 255 was registered in Dunbartonshire around 1909 and has the landaulette style of enclosed bodywork which featured a hood in the rear compartment which could be folded down as seen here if the weather permitted. This view was taken at Bannachra House by Arden on Loch Lomondside and the occupants were the Misses Brock with their chauffeur, Jamieson.

Motor trials and rallying were popular even in Edwardian times with the fortunate few who had the means to own a car. G 1025 was a 24 h.p. Albion of 1908 seen during such an event over the Cairn o' Mount hill road between Banchory and Fettercairn. At the wheel and accompanied by his family was Mr. J.F. Henderson who was a director of the Albion Motor Car Co.

Amongst the early public service vehicles built by Albion was this model A3 which was delivered in April 1906 to Edward Crosher of Dunoon for operation between there and Sandbank. It was confidently named 'Forward' in a champagne launching ceremony but served only briefly in Cowal, before passing to McKerrow's Largs and West Coast Motor Service who ran it from Largs to Wemyss Bay and to Fairlie.

1907 was the year when this 16 h.p. Albion delivery van entered service with James Taylor's Wheatholm bakery of Airdrie. It was the first motor vehicle in the fleet of horse drawn baker's carts but because of its success was soon followed by other Albions, which apparently cost less per mile to operate than the horses they replaced.

From James Taylor (Wheatholm), Ltd., Bakers, Airdrie, N.B.

WE have now had your 24 cwt. Commercial Motor given a fair trial, and so far it has never failed to deliver goods up to time and with perfect satisfaction.

We had misgivings at first as to its reliability, as it is of the first importance that our goods should arrive promptly at their destination.

These fears, however, have not been realised, and we have now every confidence that goods sent per motor van supplied by you will arrive at their destination with as much regularity as goods sent by passenger train or letters sent by post.

Yours respectfully,

JAMES TAYLOR (WHEATHOLM) LTD.

From Messrs. Malcolm Campbell, Ltd., Fruit Merchants, Glasgow.

WE have great pleasure in sending you the results of six months' running of our Albion Motor. We may state we have been agreeably surprised that we have not had a single breakdown, and have had no occasion for repairs during this time. The simplicity of the mechanism may be judged from the fact that the vehicle has been driven by one of our own vanmen for the past four months. This man's sole training consisted of one half-hour spent in practising gear-changing, after which the van was handed over to him to do its regular deliveries in and about Glasgow. We have found the van of great benefit to our business not only in giving smarter deliveries to our customers but in enabling us to extend our radius of delivery considerably. The van has delivered goods as far south as Stranraer, and frequently delivers at Bridge of Allan, Kilmacolm, etc., in all kinds of weather. We think the above speaks volumes for the reliability and solidity of our Albion Motor Van.

Yours faithfully,

MALCOLM CAMPBELL, LTD.,

DONALD CAMPBELL, *Director*.

From Messrs. J. & W. Campbell & Co., Wholesale Warehousemen, 137 Ingram Street, Glasgow.

GENTLEMEN — We have pleasure in stating that we have used two of your 16-h.p. Delivery Vans for the last twelve months. We have had them constantly on the road and they have given us every satisfaction. The mechanism is simple, which allows them to be driven by men of little experience, in fact our drivers were men in our employment who had no previous experience of motor cars.

Before we had these cars, we delivered our goods by vans drawn by horses. We find the motors do a great deal more work and give smarter deliveries.

As you know, we were so pleased with your machines that we ordered a third car which was delivered last month, and which is also giving us every satisfaction. We have now only one horsed vehicle connected with the despatch of our goods.

The 16-h.p. Traveller's Brougham, which you delivered to us last December, has been in constant use ever since and has never been stopped on the road. It has already been driven over 2,100 miles. We cannot speak too highly of the efficiency of this machine. It has proved exceedingly valuable to our traveller, enabling him to get quickly from place to place in the neighbourhood of Glasgow.

Yours faithfully,

per pro J. & W. CAMPBELL & CO.,

E. SHARMAN.

Edwardian testimonials.

The Kelso Laundry was another Scottish company which in Edwardian times replaced its horse drawn delivery fleet by Albion motor vehicles. Seen in their home town around 1910 are two 16 h.p. lorries followed by one of the horse drawn carts which they ultimately replaced. Both Albions were registered locally in Roxburghshire, the leading one being KS 160.

The grandly named Oban, Ford and Loch Awe Syndicate purchased this model A10 Albion 14 seater (SB 262) in 1911 for their tourist passenger service from Oban to connect with steamer sailings on Loch Awe. For a vehicle of that period it enjoyed quite a long life, remaining in service until 1926 when it passed to the Caledonian Steam Packet Company. It is seen here on its regular journey through the Pass of Melfort.

32-H.P. ALBION TORPEDO ⊞ ⊞ CHAR-A-BANC

	£	s	d				
CHASSIS, 25 TO 30-SEATER, 13′ 1″ Wheelbase	620	0	0	...	..	...	*Speciatif*
CHAR-A-BANC, as illustrated, to seat 25, with doors at front seat and clear passage up centre, without canopy or wind screen, upholstered in pluvinsin ...	710	0	0	...	...	...	*Spedale*
Tip-up Seats (5) fitted in centre passage	7	10	0	...	...	...	*Spedieren*
Canopy built in at rear as shown, including roll-up curtains at sides	35	0	0	...	...	...	*Spediteur*
Canopy (detachable) with canvas curtains all round and behind driver	32	5	0	...	...	...	*Spatzen*
Cape Cart Hood	35	0	0	...	...	...	*Speditivo*
Folding Wind Screen	6	5	0	...	...	...	*Spartacus*
Single Luggage Rail	3	10	0	...	..	...	*Spatroth*
Special Finish—to include hide upholstery, lino rubber on floor boards and side steps, and special finish to body	25	0	0	...	...	...	*Spatoso*

All Prices include Tyres of ample dimensions. Estimates and Drawings given for any type of Body.

For Complete Specification of Chassis and other types of Industrial Motor Vehicles, also Terms and Guarantee, see Catalogue

Specification from an Edwardian Albion catalogue which shows SD 813, a chain driven, solid tyred charabanc named 'Dreadnought' delivered to James McKerrow of Largs who operated the West Coast Motor Service (not to be confused with West Coast Motors of Campbeltown) between Fairlie, Largs and Wemyss Bay.

This photo was taken in 1911 of an export Albion which is reputed to have provided Australia's first motor mail service. Operating under contract to the Postmaster General of New South Wales, it ran between the outback mining towns of Broken Hill and Menindee. Of interest are the additional fitments for export models such as the special front wheels and the chain guard.

In 1914 the Rapid Motor Transport Co. Ltd. of Masterton St., off Keppochhill Road, Glasgow bought this chain driven 32 h.p. Albion registered G 2905 which was probably the first purpose built enclosed bus in the city. The company had intended to inaugurate bus services to districts not served by the municipal tramcars but the Great War prevented this.

A fleet of 16 h.p. Albion mail vans seen in Manchester in 1916. They were locally registered N 9543 – 9546.

During the 1914-1918 War around 6000 model A10 32 h.p. chain driven chassis were built at the Scotstoun factory for the War Department. This view shows some of these vehicles with their crews on active service in the North West Frontier of India in 1917.

A 20 h.p. 30 cwt. A16 type which was supplied in 1919 to the Hosiery Manufacturing Co. Ltd. of Irvine, Ayrshire. The signwriter has performed a fine and very appropriate job on the panels of the van, the bodywork of which was built by Robert Rogerson of Scotstoun, whose premises in Balmoral Street were adjacent to the Albion works.

In the early 1920s there were few tank wagons in use for petrol deliveries since much of it was purchased in 2 gallon cans. XP 282 was a 24 h.p. 2 tonner of 1923 used by the Anglo-American Oil Co. for distribution of these cans. It was finished in Pratt's green livery and the circular sign visible adjacent to the driver's door is the Royal "By Appointment" crest.

Harrods department store of Knightsbridge was a regular Albion customer over the years. This chain driven 2 ton van is seen at work in St. John's Park, Blackheath in the early 1920s. Many of Harrods vehicles at this period carried the equivalent of a destination board along the roof, showing their delivery area. This one reads 'Blackheath & Dartford'. According to contemporary Albion publicity, Harrods had purchased 103 Albions by 1916 and by 1920 they had 119.

Many years later, Harrods were still using Albions. Seen in London near their renowned Knightsbridge store in the mid 1950s in contrast to the upper photo is a 'Claymore' pantechnicon on furniture deliveries. This had been new to Harrods in 1954.

Contemporary Albion advertising, 1920.

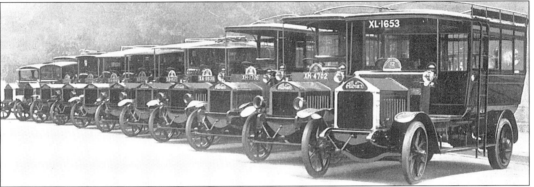

In the early 1920s, this fleet of 12 seat 20 h.p. Albion buses was in service with Charles Rickards of London on duties between the main railway stations.

Rather than choose a local Leyland, Lancashire based Coulton's Motors of Leyland, went to Glasgow in 1923 for this 32 h.p. model A10 Albion. Registered TB 5689, it was bodied by Massey Bros. of Wigan. Note that it has been fitted with pneumatic tyres at the front and solids at the rear, which was fairly common practice at that time.

Photographed with its proud driver outside the main entrance to the Albion Motors head office and works in South Street, Scotstoun prior to delivery in 1924 is MS 5051, a 24 h.p. 20 seat solid tyred charabanc bodied by John Stewart of Wishaw and supplied to Thomas Forsyth of Bannockburn for his local service between Stirling and Cowie. At this date, charabancs were becoming increasingly less common, especially for service work. The covered bus with full glazing as we know it today was normally by then a more usual choice for most operators.

The prototype 'model 26' Albion seen outside the Scotstoun works in 1925. Although little more than a year separated this vehicle from that shown above, there was a vast difference in appearance alone, with its pneumatic tyres and the attractive 28 seat bus bodywork by Northern Counties of Wigan. As a demonstrator when new, this bus made a record breaking non-stop journey from Glasgow to London and back, covering the 800-odd miles in just over a day, which was good going for 1925. It was registered HS 4086 and in its later life operated for McGill of Barrhead for a few years during the 1930s.

The normal control model 26 Albion was one of the most popular buses produced at Scotstoun, with nearly 1000 built between 1925 and 1932. HH 3318 with Northern Counties body was new in 1926 to George Hudson in the Border City of Carlisle where it is seen loading in the Market Place bus stance for Penton, a small village about 7 miles north east of Longtown, Cumbria. The driver would appear to be about to add the bicycle to the load already on the roof. Hudson's services, which included a cross-border run to Langholm in Dumfriesshire, were sold to S.M.T. of Edinburgh in 1932 in whose fleet this became A103.

Seen at the premises of R.Y. Pickering in Wishaw before delivery to Youngs' Bus Service of Paisley in 1931, this model 26 Albion was to receive the registration number AG 6550 (as it had been originally intended for their operations in Ayr) and fleet number 34 in the Y.B.S. fleet. Pickerings were better known for the construction of railway wagons and carriages and also tramcars, but from the 1920s to 1940s they additionally built bus bodies on a regular basis.

GG 9318 was the very last model 26 bus to be built and was fitted with a Cowieson body, entering service initially with John Carmichael's 'Highland' bus service in December 1932 for his Helensburgh to Glasgow route which was sold to Central S.M.T. The bus then passed to Shields of Kinlochleven and operated the service between Fort William and Tyndrum, later to be acquired by David MacBrayne with whom it continued to run until 1948.

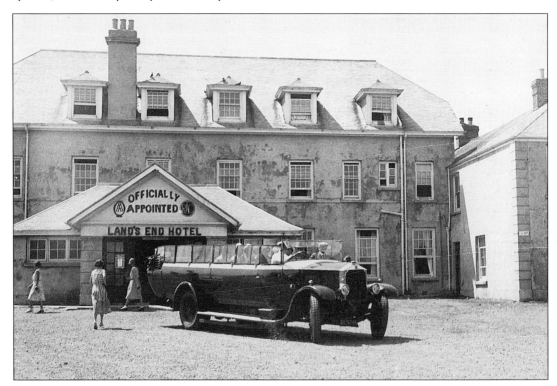

A variation on the model 26 chassis was the Albion 'Viking' coach. Vikings were introduced in 1923 and it was on this model that Albion's famous 'sunrise' badge first appeared. The name, somewhat confusingly, was given to several other models over the years, right up until the rear engined Viking of the late 1960s. This view shows a 1927 example which was one of 3 purchased by Cornish operator Hocking of Newquay. RL 5744 is seen here at Land's End after acquisition by Western National.

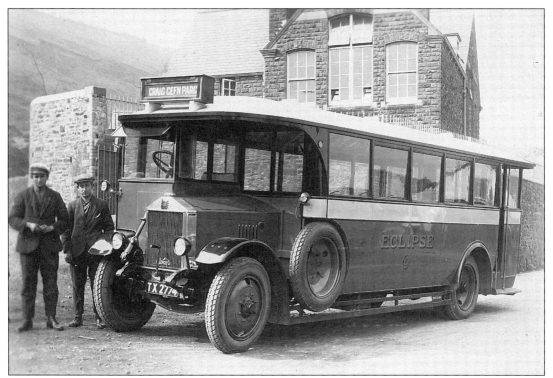

The overtype or forward control model 28 Albion had capacity to seat 32 passengers. TX 2774 was an example of this type and had bodywork by Strachan & Brown of Acton. It was delivered in 1927 to Wm. Griffiths & Sons of Craig Cefn Parc, Clydach, Glamorgan where it is seen here in the green livery of their 'Eclipse' fleet in which it was no. 3. The firm was later acquired by the Red & White company, but this particular bus had an interesting career, next being sold to Glasgow dealer Millburn Motors in 1933. It was then fitted with a new body by Forbes, Brebner & Co., of Crieff and passed to the Pitlochry Motor Co. as their no. 25. In 1939 it became D214 with Walter Alexander and later served with them as a wartime ambulance. Finally in 1945 it was sold to McInnes of Strathaven for further use as a bus.

An interesting line of four model 26 Albion Vikings and a forward control model PM28 in the 'Progress' fleet of W. Armitage of Blackpool, taken on the occasion of a visit there in 1929 by the Swansea Women's Section of the British Legion. From the left are Viking GD 5306; GD 8694, a PM28 with body by Pickering of Wishaw (these two had formerly been Albion demonstrators); FR 8085; FR 8849; FR 8931, all Vikings bodied by Burlingham & Richardson of Blackpool. In addition to their charter work, Progress also operated a service known as the 'Yorkshire Express' which connected Leeds, Bradford, Dewsbury, Huddersfield, Preston and Blackpool.

Amongst the many famous commercial fleets which operated Albions was Cadbury's Chocolate. These four solid tyred 2 ton, 24h.p. models ran in the mid 1920s from that company's Glasgow depot at Buchanan Street railway goods station. They were numbered 1-4 by Cadbury and the two on the left were registered GB 6952 and GB 7743.

A 24 h.p. Albion box van which looked somewhat antiquated even when this photo was taken shortly after it entered service in 1926. The main reason was that it was fitted all round with solid tyres which were seldom specified by this date. KA 2139 was a 30 cwt. model which ran in the 'Utopia' bread delivery fleet of George Lunt, Soho Street, Liverpool.

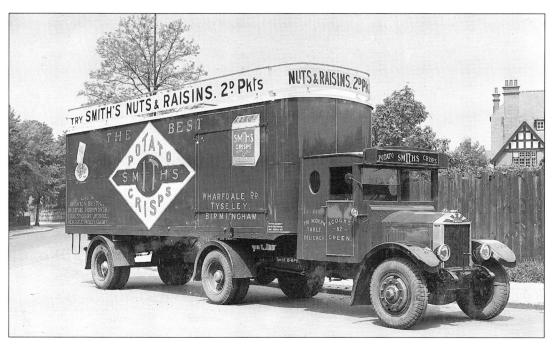

Britain's first potato crisps are reputed to have been sold in 1920 by Frank Smith, who was to become a regular Albion customer. This 1931 model was one of Smith's largest units at that time and was a 6-wheel combination with Dyson bodywork and based at the Birmingham depot in Tyseley. The company's Scottish depot was in East Lane, Paisley, which being close to my school was a natural haunt of mine, not only to see Albions but also to beg 'broken crisps'.

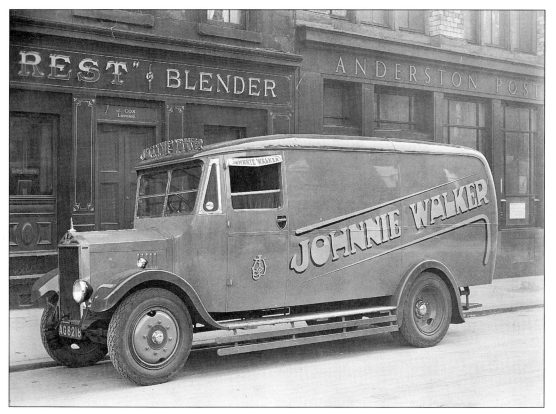

The Johnnie Walker whisky company of Kilmarnock took delivery of this smart model 41 Albion van in 1932. AG 8218 is seen on duty when still quite new at Cox's public house in Pitt Street, Glasgow, next to Anderston Post Office in an area of the city which since then has been very much redeveloped.

Looking across the Thames to Lambeth from Millbank, an Albion 4 ton tank wagon on model 50 chassis is seen passing over the newly opened Lambeth Bridge in London. YG 1303 had been purchased by the Texas Oil Company in 1932 and the bridge was officially opened in July of that year by King George V. Truck enthusiasts will also recognise GJ 9303, a Ford owned by Fry's Metal Foundries and MF 4438, a solid tyred Dennis with Schweppes table waters, both following the Texaco Albion.

An avid Albion user in the pre-war years was the Express Dairy Co. Ltd., which proudly proclaimed itself to be the largest in London. JJ 9762 entered the fleet in 1933 as their no. 153. It was a 4 ton van on model LK 51 chassis.

One of Britain's northernmost Albion operators was Robert Garden, general merchant in Kirkwall, capital of the Orkney Islands off Scotland's far north coast. In 1933 Garden took delivery of BS 1421, a 3-ton model LH 473 flat truck, seen here at Kirkwall harbour. In common with several other Scottish counties, Orkney never reached three letter index marks before its first suffix letter 'C' was introduced in January 1965.

An earlier view at the same location shows a 32 h.p. Albion in service with the Highland Park Distillery of Kirkwall, Orkney. GA 6761, registered in Glasgow, came second hand to the island in the early 1920s and is seen at the harbour unloading coal for the distillery in company with a Sentinel steam waggon. The 'K' on the funnel of the vessel shows it to be one of the Kelly line fleet, who operated colliers around the British coast.

AMD 198 was a 3 ton van supplied in 1933 by Albion's London depot in Brentfield Road, Willesden. It was no. 16 in the fleet of appropriately named R. Butcher, a carrier and contractor who was based at Smithfield meat market where this scene was taken when the vehicle was newly in service.

Albion Motors also had a depot in Old Trafford, Manchester and as a result supplied numerous models throughout Lancashire, despite the presence of Leyland Motors in the county, who of course were eventually (1951) to purchase Albion as their first acquisition. HG 1860, registered in Burnley was a 3½ ton model LH 473 double deck cattle transporter supplied in 1933 to James Allen of Hillcrest, Hapton. Amusingly a pig is being loaded and since the local phone exchange was Padiham, could this perhaps have been a delivery of Irish bacon?

Members of the Melbourne Fire Brigade proudly posing in their newly delivered fire appliance in the early 1930s soon after this special model 41 entered service in the state capital of Victoria, Australia, where Albion Motors had a local depot. The rising sun radiator on this vehicle, which has more the appearance of a large luxury automobile, is seen to good effect in this view.

Another Lancashire customer was corn merchant John Waddacor of Ashton New Road, Manchester. In 1934 his new 3½ tonner is being loaded with straw bales shortly after its delivery from the local Albion depot. Bodywork on this platform lorry was by Bond of Wythenshawe, who also built passenger vehicles.

Particularly in the 1920s and '30s, customers would request complete vehicles from Albion Motors, rather than only a chassis, which then obviously had to have a body constructed on it. Albion did not build their own bodywork, but they had a working relationship with several coachbuilders including John Mitchell of Greenock, who was also an agent for the company. Amongst the many goods and passenger bodies built by Mitchell was this 3-ton overtype lorry for James Hogg, the Cambuslang haulage contractor in 1934. Note the Greenock registration number VS 2528 which indicates the builder had registered it in his home town prior to delivery.

WG 2652 was a normal control (bonnet type) Albion model LHB463 3-tonner supplied in 1934 to the Carron Company of Falkirk which proudly bore the Royal 'By Appointment' crest on the cab doors signifying that they were ironfounders to H.M. King George V.

Publicity poster from early 1920s.

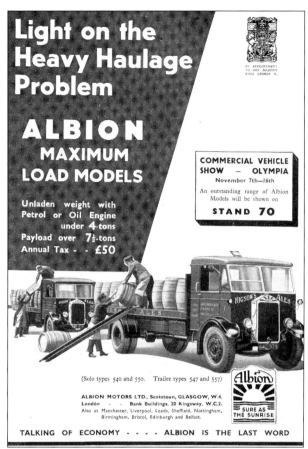

Contemporary Albion advertising from 1935 featuring commercial and passenger vehicles. The commercial advert shows lorries supplied to Higson's Brewery of Liverpool while the Cowieson bodied bus was delivered to Helen Strachan's Deeside Omnibus Service of Ballater for the Braemar to Aberdeen route and remained in service until 1958, albeit with a new post-war body by Walker of Aberdeen.

In 1935 this impressive 6-wheeler model 58 type was specially built to the specification of the Italian Government and was fitted with a mobile water distilling plant which had been constructed by engineers G.& J. Weir of Cathcart. It is seen descending Gardner Street, Partick, which has one of the steepest gradients in Glasgow and was accordingly often used on official test drives of Albion vehicles from the nearby Scotstoun works.

Another 6-wheeler supplied in 1935. This was a model RL59 12 tonner purchased by the Caledonian Omnibus Co. of Dumfries for their haulage division, although as may be seen also bore the name of James Bell who had been a haulage contractor based in Dunragit, Wigtownshire. Although Caledonian had acquired Bell's business in 1934, the name was retained for goodwill purposes for quite some time. OS 3890 was the Wigtownshire registration number allocated to this vehicle, which had a Gardner 6LW diesel, or oil engine as it was more commonly known at that time. Its bodywork was by Rogerson of Scotstoun.

Co-operative Societies throughout the land tended to use Albions in preference to most other makes of vehicle. The Greenock Central Co-operative Society Ltd. of Roxburgh Street, Greenock, was no exception and in this scene are six of their fleet which from the left are VS 2865, 2863, 3011, 3181, 3010 and 2867, all dating from 1935/1936. The two 5-ton K530 models on the left were fitted with Gardner 4LW diesel engines, while the remainder were all petrol powered. Note the Greenock Co-op emblem of the 'green oak' which was displayed beside the cab doors of every member of the fleet.

YJ 4513 was a 6-wheel model RL559 Albion 13-tonner supplied to Dundee haulage contractor D. Horsburgh via the local agent McAra of Dundee. Prior to delivery it appeared at the Scottish Motor Show at the Glasgow Kelvin Hall in November 1936 on the stand of J. Brockhouse & Co., who built the bodywork.

Haulage contractor Hutch Smith of Canonbie, Dumfriesshire, used CSM 312 for milk collection purposes around the farming area of his local community. It was a model KL 127 4½ tonner of 1937 and is seen sporting an A.A. badge on its radiator.

Albions were not so commonly used by local authority cleansing departments but two Scottish towns which proved exceptions were Paisley and St. Andrews. In the upper view we see XS 3919, a gully emptier purchased by Paisley Corporation in 1936 but the scene itself was taken during wartime as may be noticed by the regulation masked headlamp and the white rimmed mudguards. The lower photo shows CSP 474 which was a more conventional bin lorry delivered to St. Andrews town council in 1938 and was bodied in Fife by John Jackson of Dunfermline.

SH 5523 was a model T 561 8-wheel 15-tonner supplied with cab built by Jackson of Dunfermline in 1937 to Wm. Rodger & Sons Ltd., Williambank, Earlston, Berwickshire, a prominent haulage contractor at that time, with other depots in Glasgow, Edinburgh, Leith, Newcastle and London. It is seen here en route from Goole in Yorkshire to Rosyth in Fife with a load of steel tanks.

Illustrations of Motor Shows are invariably fascinating because they are packed with interest. This view of the Albion stand at the 1937 Earls Court Exhibition in London shows some of the then current commercial and passenger vehicle range on display. Prominent in the foreground is CAX 395 a 'Valkyrie' coach supplied to regular Albion customer Red & White of Chepstow, while the 'Victor' behind it is BV 8221 with Cronshaw of Hendon. Both carried Duple coachwork. The lorries include 6 tonners for the Gas Light & Coke Co. (ELC 529) and the L.M.S. Railway. Also visible are two Daimler 'deckers on the Weymann stand, a rare twin-steer Leyland 'Gnu' which went to Alexander of Falkirk and in the lower right corner a neat little Dennis 'Ajax' lorry.

The Scottish Motor Shows held at the Glasgow Kelvin Hall always combined displays of both private cars and commercials, which to many visitors proved of greater interest and variety than the current separate shows. Albion's stand at the 1938 venue showed the chassis of a 15 ton eight-wheeler, a 2 ½ ton bonnet type destined for Robb Bros. of Arbroath and a flat lorry for Ferguson of Ayr (CS 8688). The Pickering bodied coach was CS 8680, a CX 9 'Valkyrie', supplied to Dodds of Troon.

The only Albion in the fleet of Ezra Laycock, Cowling, Yorkshire, was WW 8139 a model 24 type with 20 seat bodywork by Barnaby of Hull, which was new in 1928 to this company which claimed to have operated the first bus in Yorkshire. It is seen en route from Barnoldswick to Skipton negotiating the twisting road alongside the Leeds & Liverpool Canal. In 1972 the business was acquired by Pennine Motor Services, Gargrave.

In 1929 this 'Viking-six' model with Alexander bodywork was supplied to Messrs. Mullen & Thompson (Northern) of Elgin, passing to Walter Alexander of Falkirk in 1931. In 1932 this and seven sister buses were returned to Albion Motors where they were refurbished and then sold. SO 3578 and two others found homes in Northern Ireland, this one with David Lawther of Drumbeg, Dunmurry. It is seen in his attractive livery of two shades of blue in College Square, Belfast. In 1935 it was acquired by the Northern Ireland Road Transport Board, with whom it served for a further two years.

Albion advertising of 1931 featuring a 'Viking-six' which was one of several in the large fleet of Young's Bus Service of Paisley. Bodywork on these PMB 28 chassis was supplied by Northern Counties of Wigan.

Amongst the smaller Albion passenger vehicles was this 14 seat bus on a special LB 41 goods chassis. It was purchased in 1930 by Mr. Wood of Riddings, a member of the Association service which ran to Ripley in Derbyshire where this bus was registered RB 432.

Also new in 1930 was FM 6014 which was one of six similar Northern Counties bodied 20 seater buses purchased by Crosville Motor Services for use on routes which crossed the Menai Bridge to the Isle of Anglesey, where no. 401 was photographed bound for Llangefni from Bangor. At that time there was a restriction on the bridge which precluded the use of larger buses, hence the use of this special model LC 24 Albion with 12' 9" wheelbase.

Northern Ireland was home to many Albions in the early 1930s. For example AZ 9546 was one of a fleet of 24 identical 'Valkyries' delivered to the Great Northern Railway Co., of Belfast in 1932 and all had 30 seat bodies by Weymann of Addlestone. No. 248 is seen on the Lisburn Road, bound for Lurgan via Flatfield.

The L.M.S. Railway (Northern Counties Committee) in Belfast also operated a large Albion fleet. These seven model PH 49 'Victors' were supplied to the company in 1933 and all carried 20 seat bodywork built at Walter Alexander's Drip Road coachworks in Stirling. They were registered CZ 2010-2016.

Similar to those in the previous illustration were three 20 seat 'Victors' supplied in 1933 to Hebble Motor Services of Halifax and numbered 93-95. These, however, differed in having bodywork by Eastern Counties of Lowestoft. This scene at Myrtle Park, Bingley, shows no. 95 about to leave the stop at the Myrtle Dairy for Halifax on the hourly service via Cullingworth and Denholme.

Hebble were staunch Albion supporters. As such, in addition to the 'Victors' of 1933, 'Valiants' and 'Valkyries' were also purchased that year. One of the latter is seen bound for Burnley on Heptonstall Moor between Colden and Jack Bridge on the lengthy Blackshaw Head route from Leeds and Halifax. This service 15 was normally operated by Leyland Titan 'deckers from Leeds to Halifax where an Albion saloon would be waiting with the onward connection to Burnley – on this occasion JX 505 (no. 98) with 32 seat bodywork by Brush of Loughborough.

An Albion 'Valiant' with 32 seat bodywork by Cowieson of Glasgow delivered in 1933 to the unusually named 'Radio Service' operated on the Culter to Dyce route by Raffan of Woodside, Aberdeen. This firm sold out to Walter Alexander in 1935 and RG 3692 became their E21 for three years before sale to Carmichael of Glenboig who kept it until wartime when it was next sold to Belfast based Northern Ireland Road Transport Board, who re-registered it as GZ 308.

A peep beneath the bonnet of a 1934 'Valiant' in the fleet of Young's Bus Service of Paisley revealing the 38/75 h.p. Albion-Ricardo diesel engine.

Outside the premises of Glasgow coachbuilder F.D. Cowieson in Charles Street, St. Rollox prior to delivery in 1936 to the Highland Transport Company of Inverness (not to be confused with Carmichael's much more southerly Highland Bus Service of Glenboig, Lanarkshire) are two model PW 141 'Valkyries'. ST 8652/3 endured to be absorbed into Highland Omnibuses fleet when it was formed in 1952 as the youngest member of the Scottish Bus Group. The attractive bodywork was enhanced by Highland's crimson and ivory livery incorporating their impressive crest of a swooping golden eagle. The general manager's name was equally impressive: Wilmot Hanbury Fowke.

Two Albion 'Victors' in the appropriately named 'Victor' bus and sun saloon coach service owned by Daniel Ferguson of Renfrew. HS 7019 was a normal control model PHC 49 with 24 seat rear entrance bus bodywork by Cadogan of Perth new in 1933 while forward control HS 8208 was a PK 115 model of 1935 with 30 seat Cowieson coachwork. The Ferguson family had previously owned the 'Victoria' bus service based in Renfrew and later at Inchinnan where the present day Arriva depot was built by the family before acquisition by Western S.M.T. in the early 1930s.

Albion had been doing nicely on the export market over the years, particularly to colonial countries where depots had been established. Early in 1936, seven model 115 'Victors' were shipped from the Royal Albert Dock on the Thames aboard the British India Line vessel *Matiana* to Mombasa for operation with Kenya Bus Services. Five were 32 seaters, as seen here and two had 24 seats, all built by Duple Motor Bodies of Hendon. The forward compartment had space for 14 first class passengers while the unglazed section to the rear held 18 in second class accommodation.

It's "pence per mile" that counts—

—and the remarkable figures obtained by users of the **ALBION 'VICTOR'** are due not only to its outstanding economy and small maintenance charges but also to its low first cost.

CHASSIS PRICES:
(ex Works)

24/26 Passenger **£490**

30/32 Passenger **£500**

ALBION MOTORS LTD.,
SCOTSTOUN, GLASGOW, W.4.

London : Bank Buildings, 20, Kingsway, W.C.2.

Also at Manchester, Liverpool, Leeds, Sheffield, Nottingham, Lincoln, Norwich, Birmingham, Bristol, Edinburgh, and Belfast.

ALBIONS CUT THE COSTS AND RAISE THE PROFITS

Albion 'Victor' VD 7003 which was owned by Isaac Hutchison of Overtown features in this advert from 1937. Coachwork on this PK 115 model was by John Stewart of Wishaw.

DPU 746 was a model PV141 'Valkyrie' fitted with Albion's 6 cylinder petrol engine and delivered in 1937 to Thomas Webster of Laindon, Essex, who operated under the fleet name of 'Old Tom'. 32 seat coachwork by Strachans of Acton was fitted. Here we see it in Romford picking up passengers for Clacton.

The six wheeler model 145 'Valkyrie', with a 19' wheelbase and 30' length allowed greater seating capacity than was then considered normal. The largest fleet of this type of Albion was operated by Young of Paisley who had no fewer than fifteen with 39 seat Cowieson bodywork delivered in 1937/8. This view shows the only example to have been fitted with coachwork by Burlingham of Blackpool. It was a 37 seater owned by Fieldsend of Salford and registered RJ 7576 in 1937.

The most numerous of the 'Valkyrie ' models were the CX 9, 11 and 13 types, with no fewer than 823 built between their introduction in 1938 and demise in 1951. JMC 271 was an early example of a CX 9, which used the 4 cylinder engine and was delivered in 1938 to McEwen's A.& W. Hire Service of Harrow. Albions carried a wide variety of different makes of bodywork and this particular one was an unusually styled 33 seat coach built by Mulliner of Northampton who also had a fine reputation for their luxury car bodies.

Apart from four model A 10 Albions fitted with open top deck bodywork providing total seating for 34 (the capacity of a midi-bus today!) and operated by Newcastle Corporation shortly after the 1914-18 war, Albion's first proper venture into building a double deck chassis did not happen until 1932. It was appropriately christened the 'Venturer' and proved to be a steady seller over its 20 years of production. Apart from an experimental chassis, GG 8742 was the first 'Venturer' (M 80 type) and is shown here with its 51 seat Cowieson body finished in the livery of Glasgow Corporation Transport passing the G.C.T. head office in Bath Street at the Renfield Street corner. It operated with them on demonstration for a period before sale to Young's Bus Service of Paisley (see p. 41) who went on to place a large fleet in service. Glasgow's own first 'Venturer' was not purchased until 1935.

Albion Motors' first customer for their new 'Venturer' model was West Wales Motors Ltd. of LLanelli, Carmarthenshire, who made the purchase in February 1933. This was TH 3293, which was numbered 10 in their fleet and had lowbridge bodywork reputedly built by Strachans. It looks most attractive in its grey livery with red bands, but despite being very new, had already suffered a dent just below the upper front nearside window. In 1942 the body was replaced by Duple and a diesel engine took the place of the original 6 cylinder petrol unit.

Another early 'Venturer' of 1933 was US 1214 which initially served as a demonstrator, but was soon purchased by Walter Alexander of Falkirk in whose fleet it was numbered E19 and later RO87. This was a 48 seater with lowbridge type bodywork by Northern Counties and a Beardmore diesel engine which was replaced by an Albion diesel in 1936. It ran for much of its life at Alexander's Milngavie depot, operating there until withdrawal from service in 1955.

Young's Bus Service of Paisley was one of Albion's best customers. This atmospheric scene was taken in 1934 inside the almost cathedral-like Y.B.S. garage in Mary Street, Johnstone which had previously been an engineering works. Driving from the garage to take up service are two particularly interesting vehicles, the first being GG 9461 which was to remain unique as the only Albion six-wheel 'decker and which received the model name 'Valorous'. Following it is previously illustrated GG 8742, the original 'Venturer' production model. This had Cowieson bodywork whereas the 'Valorous' was bodied by Pickering of Wishaw. Other Y.B.S. Albions in the background include model 26 and 28 saloons and another 'Venturer' 'decker.

Baillie Brothers of Hartfield Garage, Dumbarton operated nine Albion 'Venturers' on their busy service between Glasgow, Dumbarton and Balloch. SN 6294 was the first of seven Cowieson bodied examples delivered in 1934. Two years later the company sold out to Central S.M.T. and this bus became C1 in the fleet, where it remained at their Gavinburn depot, Old Kilpatrick, until withdrawal and sale to Millburn Motors in 1949. It is seen here prior to leaving the Albion works, where it had to undergo the 'tilt test' to satisfy Ministry of Transport regulations.

Three reasons for ALBION Supremacy

1. EXCELLENCE of design

2. EXCELLENCE of workmanship

3. EXCELLENCE of performance

Resulting in More Miles for your Money.

"SURE AS THE SUNRISE"

Range of Albion Passenger Models 24 to 60 seats.

Heavy-Oil or Petrol Engines

Albion
ALBION MOTORS LTD.
SCOTSTOUN, GLASGOW, W.4.
London : Bank Buildings, 20 Kingsway, W.C.2.
Also at Manchester, Liverpool, Leeds, Nottingham, Sheffield, Birmingham, Bristol, Edinburgh and Belfast.

Albion 'Venturer.'   Albion 'Valkyrie.'   Albion 'Victor.'

See the Albion Exhibit, STAND 71, Scottish Motor Show, Glasgow, Nov. 16-24

1934 advertising which publicised the Scottish Motor Show at Kelvin Hall, Glasgow, depicting a 'Venturer', a 'Valkyrie' and a 'Victor'. The 'Venturer' was US 7808 which carried a 55 seat lowbridge Northern Counties body and which after a period working as a demonstration vehicle with Albion was sold to Graham of Kirkintilloch. When Alexander acquired this company in 1938 it received their number RO229 and was later transferred to the associated David Lawson fleet. It ended its life working for Blair & Palmer of Carlisle from 1945-1949.

A 1938 delivery to Young of Paisley was XS 4770 which was one of six 'Venturer' CX 19 types with Preston-built English Electric bodywork. This was 109 in Young's fleet, to be renumbered 2109 by Western S.M.T. when Y.B.S. was acquired in 1951. It is seen on their frequent Glasgow/Paisley/Johnstone service at the Thorn, between Elderslie and Johnstone.

Glasgow Corporation Transport Department operated more Albion 'Venturers' than anyone else – 268 in total purchased between 1935 and 1953. This was one of fifteen CX 19 models delivered in 1938, all of which had highbridge 56 seat bodies by Cowieson of St. Rollox, Glasgow. These in fact were the last from that builder, ending an association which went back to the original Corporation buses of 1924. The first Albion single decks for G.C.T. in 1927 also had Cowieson bodies. No. 629, with the very appropriate Glasgow registration BUS 195 is seen at Anniesland Cross, closely followed by a more elderly A.E.C. Regent, both operating service 2 to Knightswood.

The Lanarkshire independent Isaac Hutchison of Overtown (one of very few old-established operators still in business today) purchased this CX 19 'Venturer' in 1939. AVA 935 featured the unusual combination of an Albion 'decker with highbridge 56 seat bodywork on Cowieson framework by local firm John Stewart of neighbouring Wishaw, whose Coltness Coachworks are visible behind.

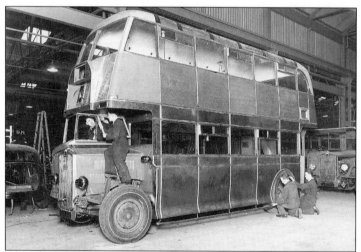

With the onset of World War Two in 1939, Albion's core business was forced into a compulsory change. Instead of buses and trucks for the civilian market, Albion employees found themselves producing a range of military vehicles for the Ministry of Supply. Even such diverse items as service revolvers and torpedo engines were manufactured. However, it was to be 1942 when the last bus chassis left Scotstoun before a four year gap until after the war. DGB 437/8 were two of ten wartime CX 19 'Venturers' supplied in 1942 to Glasgow Corporation, who built their own bodywork on eight, including 789/90, seen during construction at Larkfield bus works. The regulation wartime masked headlamps have already been fitted.

Production of the 'Venturer' CX 19 resumed after the war. In 1948 EAV 161 was delivered to north-east independent Cruikshank & Ross of Newburgh, Aberdeenshire and locally built bodywork was constructed by Walker of Aberdeen. In 1949 the owners sold out to James Sutherland of Peterhead, who in turn sold to Alexander in 1950, giving the bus three liveries in as many years. Here it is towards the end of its life in 1959 in final guise working as RO670 from Alexander's depot in Cowdenbeath, Fife, being followed by two Guy Arabs while en route to Stevenson's Beath.

Sales of Albions in general and 'Venturers' in particular to Australia were particularly buoyant after the war ended in 1945. The Department of Government Transport in New South Wales purchased 143 'Venturers' between 1947 and 1949, making it the biggest post-war customer for this type (Glasgow Corporation came close second with 138). Seen in Wynyard Square, Sydney shortly after delivery in 1948 is M.O. 2003 which appropriately had local Clyde-built bodywork with dual doorways as originally specified. It would appear that some mechanical problem warranted close inspection.

One immediately associates the Harbour Bridge with Sydney. Seen in the late 1940s is a long line of Albion 'Venturers' battling their way across the bridge to the city terminus at Wynyard from a variety of the northside suburbs. As in the other view, the two leaders of this line were bodied by the Clyde Engineering Works of Sydney. A number of these 'deckers remained in service until the early 1970s and several were then sold on for further years of independent bus work which was a real tribute to their builders, whose motto of course was 'Sure as the Sunrise'.

The only member of the Scottish Bus Group to purchase new Albion 'Venturers' was Western S.M.T. of Kilmarnock, which took two CX 19s in 1947 and sixteen CX 37s in 1949. CSD 877, one of the latter, was based at Ayr depot and regularly operated the long (90 miles) route between Glasgow and Stranraer on which it is seen here at Eastwood Toll. All this batch had lowbridge 53 seat bodywork by Alexander.

The final 'Venturer' models featured Albion's larger 9.9 litre engine and were designated CX 37 type, appearing in 1949. The very last of the line were twenty five Weymann bodied examples placed in service by Glasgow Corporation in 1953 and B137 is seen squeezing past B138 while testing a proposed new service in the city's eastern suburbs. This view distinctly shows the final version of the 'Venturer' radiator and when this bus is compared with the original 'Venturers' of twenty years before, it is easy to see why Albion had the reputation of being conservative to the point of old-fashioned in their outlook and general design.

The 'Venturer' was not quite the last double deck model to carry the Albion name. In 1961 the Scotstoun factory commenced production of the 'Lowlander' which carried bodywork with capacity for a maximum of 72 seats, but only the first four prototype 'Lowlander' chassis were completely manufactured by Albion, as the following 270 production chassis were assembled at Scotstoun using kits supplied by Leyland. This explains why examples supplied to English operators carried Leyland badges whilst those for Scottish customers were badged 'Albion'. UCS 646 is a typical Alexander bodied 'Lowlander' LR1 model, with pneumocyclic semi-automatic gearbox which had been new to Western S.M.T. in 1963 and passed in 1976 to Alexander (Northern) of Aberdeen where it is seen in Market Street.

The Lowlander chassis was specially designed for use with a low height (13' 6") double deck body, having a single step forward entrance controlled by the driver. This is another Alexander bodied example which was part of the first order for an English operator. 162 NVO was supplied in November 1962 to East Midland Motor Services at Chesterfield as their D162. It was an LR 7 model with conventional Leyland synchromesh gearbox but unusually for a customer south of the border carries Albion and not Leyland badging.

Continuing again with commercials, brewers throughout the country were good customers for Albion products. Seen on delivery work outside the Humber Hotel in Grimsby is AEE 577, a 7-ton CX 1 type lorry purchased in 1947 by Hewitt's Grimsby Ales.

A similar scene but this time in Rotherham, home of Bentley's Brewery who owned EET 476, a 5-ton model FT 3 Albion, new in 1948. Its unladen weight was 2 tons 19 cwts., which legally allowed it to enjoy the benefit of the 30 m.p.h. speed limit then in force. Had it tipped the scales, however, with an unladen weight which exceeded 3 tons then its speed would have accordingly been limited to 20 m.p.h.

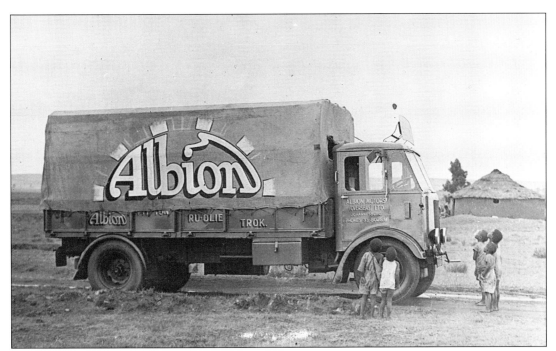

In the post-war years Albions continued their pre-war success, particularly in colonial countries where local depots and agencies had been founded. A journey for publicity purposes was made from Johannesburg in November 1948 across South Africa using this FT 3L model for demonstration. The local children at a wayside native village appear to be suitably impressed.

Textile manufacturers Gladstone's of Galashiels placed this 6 cylinder petrol model FT 3 in service in 1949. The stylish van bodywork by Kirkness & Innes of Leith (now trading as K & I Coachworks and who celebrated their centenary in 1998) was quite impressive with its chrome accessories and the end result could perhaps be described as being the equivalent to a 'GT' model of its time. LS 5186 was locally registered in Selkirkshire and is seen here outside imposing Melville Castle, Midlothian.

A pre-delivery view of an eight-wheel HD 57L model of the early 1950s which was owned by the nationalised haulage organisation British Road Services. It was operated by the Scottish Parcels Group from the former Young's Express Deliveries depot in Portman Street, Glasgow.

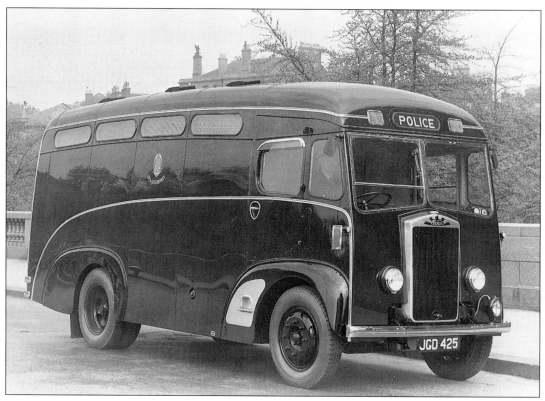

JGD 425 was a 4 cylinder petrol powered FT 21 type in service from May 1951 as a City of Glasgow Police prison van, locally bodied by Croft of Gallowgate, who also built a number of double deck bodies on Albion 'Venturer' chassis for Glasgow Corporation. This van had the doubtful reputation of having transported murderer Peter Manuel to and from Barlinnie Prison and finally to his execution there. In 1962 it was sold to the Endrick Dairy in Hopehill Road and converted to a travelling shop. It still exists today in the care of a preservationist.

A 1951 Albion 'Chieftain' hard at work in Sheffield, employed by the Hallamshire Steel & File Co. Ltd. The 'Chieftain' range of models, with sturdy but economic 4 cylinder oil engines, had been introduced in 1948 and quickly proved to be popular best sellers.

KGA 613 was a model FT 101 'Clydesdale' tipper of 1952 working with quarrymasters and brickmakers the Alexandra Transport Company Ltd., of Alexandra Parade, Glasgow.

A near neighbour of Albion Motors in Scotstoun was the Blythswood Shipbuilding Co. whose 'Chieftain' KGA 309 of 1952 is dwarfed by a vessel on the stocks.

A 'Chieftain' tipper (FAG 443) of 1953 bodied by Autolifts of Lancashire and owned by the National Coal Board with whom it was based in their East Ayr area at Lugar, near Cumnock.

The Salvage Corps of the Glasgow Fire Service used this special FT 3 model from 1953. It is seen outside their headquarters and base in Ingram Street, Glasgow.

Amongst Albion's best customers in Scotland was the Co-operative movement. The Scottish Co-operative Wholesale Society transport department in Scotland Street, Glasgow was the concessionaire for all Albions supplied to Co-ops. throughout Scotland. In addition much of the bodywork, including that on this 'Claymore' van of 1954, was built at the S.C.W.S. transport department coachworks in Rutherglen.

A 1954 example of the popular model FT 37 'Chieftain' with 4 cylinder Albion diesel engine. NWU 327 was owned by wholesale potato merchant Hall of Hoyland near Barnsley and is seen delivering to a fish and chip shop only a short distance from the local Albion depot in Beulah Road, Owlerton, Sheffield.

'Claymores' across the border were historically more often associated with the raids by Scottish reivers on their unfortunate Northumbrian neighbours. This 'Claymore', however, was of Albion manufacture and was bought in 1954 by Newcastle Breweries. VBB 171 was no. 3 in their fleet and is seen delivering to the Wheat Sheaf Hotel in Ponteland Road, near Newcastle Airport.

53

Paisley fruit and vegetable merchant Thomas Colquhoun purchased XS 8974, an underfloor engined 'Claymore' in 1954. Contemporary Albion advertising described this model as having 'revolutionary new cab design, with seating for 3, a low unobstructed floor and easy access.' This view shows it in its youth while delivering to Mrs. Brown's general store in Orchard Street, Paisley. The 'Claymore' was later claimed to be Britain's most successful underfloor engined commercial vehicle and remained in production until 1965.

USM 415 was a 'Chieftain' of 1956 which entered service with T.C. Brown & Co., of Lochmaben, Dumfriesshire and seen with a load of barrels containing imported mutton tallow from New Zealand. Brown's business was sold to Curries of Dumfries.

A 1959 model CL 3L 5-ton 'Claymore' with pantechnicon body supplied to Meikle & McKellar the removal company from the Isle of Bute whose familiar slogan 'Royal Rothesay' was always applied to their bright liveried red and yellow vans. Bute was one of several Scottish counties whose motor licensing numbers never climbed high because of the area's low population. This was SJ 2041 and by 1964 when suffix letters were introduced, Bute's series had still not topped 3000.

Young Bros. of Galston ran this 1960 'Clydesdale' with LAD cab on milk collection work around farms in Ayrshire. The 1750 gallon milk tank was by Butterfield of Shipley, Yorkshire. Young's operations were taken over by Jas. McKinnon Jnr. of Kilmarnock in 1962.

Millburn Motors of Glasgow were concessionaires for Albion Motors and also built commercial vehicle bodies. Their adverts would regularly appear in the pages of the 'Leyland Journal' after Albion became a member of the Leyland group. This one appeared in 1963, a year after Glasgow withdrew its municipal tramway system and featured WUS 875 a 1959 'Clydesdale' tipper supplied to the Alexandra Transport Co. (now Tilcon). The scene of track removal is in Dumbarton Road, Scotstoun and in the background is one of the Leyland 'Atlanteans' which replaced the trams and which carried the familiar Albion saltire badges purely as a public relations exercise.

Pit props or pulp would have been the final products from these logs being loaded to Albion Super Reiver FSB 105E which was no. 4 in the fleet of McNab & Weir of Strachur on Loch Fyne. This scene dates from 1967 when the new truck was operating under contract to Cowal-Ari sawmills, in the Argyll National Forest Park. A Hiab crane was fitted to make loading easier as each log weighs about 4 cwt.

Back to the buses and continuing after the 1939-45 War when Albion's full range of passenger vehicles again became available, we see an example of a model CX 9 'Valkyrie', delivered in 1947 to John Carmichael's 'Highland' bus service of Glenboig, Lanarkshire. CVD 747 was the only bus ever built by Love & Maxwell of Glenboig and apparently the 39 seat wooden body was really too heavy for the 4 cylinder engine, producing a performance which was best described as "sluggish" by the owners and something altogether alternative by the drivers!

Another CX 9 'Valkyrie' but this time with coach body as opposed to a service bus. This example was delivered to McKelvie of Barrhead in 1948. Although this haulage company was perhaps better known for its large lorry fleet they also operated a few coaches on charter and tour work. DHS 610 was a 33 seater built by the Junction Motor Body Works, of Manchester.

DHS 826 was a Duple bodied Albion 'Victor' FT 3 which started life in 1949 as a demonstration vehicle before purchase by Morrison of Lochwinnoch, Renfrewshire. It then passed to Rothesay Motor Services on the island of Bute, with whom it is seen in the late 1950s at the terminus of their route to Canada Hill. This company replaced its original 6 cylinder petrol engine with a 4 cylinder diesel.

Five of a fleet of twenty two 'Valkyrie' 4-cylinder CX 9 models destined for Accra, capital of the Gold Coast of West Africa (now Ghana) in 1948. Alongside is a 6-cylinder CX 13 for A1 Service member McPhail of Irvine on the Clyde Coast of West Scotland. All were bodied by Brockhouse of Livingston Street, Clydebank, the location of this pre-delivery scene. Close inspection of the African buses reveals the fascinating destinations CHORKO; ZONGO; MANPROB; ADABRAKA and ACCRA.

Another African customer in the 1940s and '50s was the East African Railways & Harbours Board in Tanganyika (now Tanzania) who operated a large fleet of Albion 'Victors'. Wogogo tribesmen are seen on the rough road in the hinterland between Dodomo and Iringa boarding one of a batch of FT 39 models delivered in 1954. Bodywork was by Brockhouse (South Africa) which was associated with the British Brockhouse company.

Albion commercial and passenger vehicles had been operated by various owners on the island of Skye since 1912. The Skye Transport Company and its predecessors purchased a variety of buses over a 20 year span and this scene shows one of six similar models delivered between 1948 and 1950. By this time ownership was controlled by the Scottish Co-operative Wholesale Society Ltd. who built the 20 seat bodywork on the AZ 9 goods chassis in their own premises in Rutherglen. GGA 989 is seen in 1954 on the then indifferent main road connecting the island capital of Portree with the ferry port at Kyleakin. Skye Transport was acquired by David MacBrayne in 1958 and this bus became their no. 17 for a short period before conversion to lorry no. 2 for which purpose the chassis had been originally intended.

Travel stained at Lairg post office after its near 60 mile journey from the village of Durness on the far north-west coast we see NS 2392 which was one of a pair of 'Victors' supplied in 1950 to the Sutherland Transport & Trading Company which had been operating Albions since the Edwardian era (see p. 4). Since these lengthy rural services additionally involved the carriage of mail and parcels, their buses incorporated compartments at the back especially for this purpose.

This 6 cylinder 'Valiant' CX 39 was one of three similar Duple bodied examples delivered to well known coach proprietors Dodds' of Troon in 1949.

In 1950, Cotter's Tours of Glasgow purchased three Albion 'Valiants' with full fronted coach bodies by Plaxton of Scarborough. The styling covered their traditional Albion radiators and successfully disguised their origins, making for a more modern appearance which was entirely in keeping with the Cotter image for Continental touring work. This one in the striking black and orange livery, complete with the additional embellishment of triple air horns on the roof, was registered HGE 862.

Only two model KP 71 Albion buses were built, both with 9.7 litre 8 cylinder engines and both received bodywork by Scottish Aviation at Prestwick Airport in 1952. One was a 30 seat coach version which ran between Glasgow and London for Western S.M.T. while the other was this 39 seat rear entrance/front exit bus in the fleet of Glasgow Corporation. Numbered BS1 it was naturally nicknamed 'Bessie' and is seen on a Clydebank local service at Linnvale terminus. It was withdrawn after only 7 years service.

The Channel Islands of Jersey and Guernsey both used Albion Victors in their fleets. Seen here is an impressive delivery of FT 39 models with 4 cylinder diesel engines which was made to the Guernsey Railway Company in the mid 1950s. All carried 35 seat bodywork by Heaver of Durrington, Wiltshire.

Albion 'Victors' were popular at home and away. In the far east, Kowloon Motor Bus Services took a batch of no less than 100 similar to this in 1963 which brought their total in service up to 200 at that time. Dual door bodywork by Metal Sections of Oldbury with 42 seat capacity (plus 17 standing) was supplied in C.K.D. form and assembled by K.M.B. in Hong Kong. This model VT 23 type awaits departure time for Kowloon at the Tai O Mun terminus at Clearwater Bay.

In 1955, Albion introduced their 'Nimbus' model MR 9, specifically intended for rural or lightly trafficked bus routes. These were ideal for the territory in Co. Donegal served by the Lough Swilly services and this company purchased three of each of this and the later NS 3 model between 1957 and 1960, all 31 seaters bodied in Ireland by O'Doherty of Lifford. Seen here in Rathmullan is ZP 4244 (no. 90) which was the first to arrive.

Another example of the fuel frugal, lightweight, underfloor engined 'Nimbus'. This one was supplied in 1957 to Southampton Corporation and was fitted with Alexander bodywork.

The Albion 'Aberdonian' MR 11 introduced in 1957 was really a larger version of the 'Nimbus', with a chassis suitable for 30' x 8' bodywork, as on this 41 seat Plaxton bodied example new that year to regular Albion customer John Carmichael of Glenboig. In 1966, Carmichael's 'Highland' fleet was sold to Alexander (Midland) when this coach then became MNL 20 until withdrawal in 1972. Leyland's mid-mounted small 6-cylinder 0.350 power unit fitted to 'Aberdonians' tended to cause complaints of insufficient power from drivers, although owners enjoyed their enhanced economy.

The Scottish Bus Group ordered relatively few of the 'Aberdonian' model (so named for its frugal characteristics and particularly low fuel consumption). For example, Western S.M.T. of Kilmarnock purchased only three, all of which passed to fellow group member Alexander (Northern) in 1965. This official view in the lee of Stirling Castle shows KCS 424 after leaving Alexander's nearby coachworks in Drip Road before their move to Falkirk. It entered service in 1957 based at Newton Mearns depot, from where it often operated the Glasgow-Lancashire services.

Forty years after the first 'Viking' model was introduced in 1923, Albion produced yet another, which was displayed at the 1963 Scottish Motor Show in Glasgow. This view shows the prototype VK 41 chassis, with engine mounted at the front, on test in the rugged Trossachs countryside. It was bodied by Alexander and registered BWG 650B, entering service with Alexander (Midland) on trial for a year before returning to Albion Motors. Ultimately it ran for several years with Lochs Motor Transport on the Island of Lewis.

Flashback to a 'Viking' of the 1920s. ST 4066 was an 18 seat Cowieson bodied model PF 26 charabanc purchased by Inverness & District Motor Services and which became no. 29 in the subsequent Highland Transport fleet when it was formed in 1930. It is seen on tour at Dornie, Wester Ross during its first season's work in 1926. Close inspection of the original photograph shows the restriction sign 'speed 12 m.p.h.' painted behind the front wing above the running board.

In 1965, the re-designed 'Viking' was revealed with its engine at the rear and classified as the VK 43. Apparently designed in collaboration with the Scottish Bus Group, it was natural that all the Group companies (except Western) should place orders. This advert from 1968 features Alexander (Midland) MNV 21 which was one of 9 with Alexander/Potter bodies built in Belfast. 75 'Vikings' were delivered to 'Midland' between 1965 and 1969. Note the current company logo at that time.

63

The 1967 Scottish Motor Show, where we notice Albion on an adjacent stand to Leyland and A.E.C. since all were members of the same group by this time. The uninspiring circular logo adopted by Leyland can be seen on either side of the Albion name. Prominent is a 13½ ton gross 'Chieftain'/Edbro tipper with standard L.A.D. (Leyland/Albion/Dodge) cab in front of a Super Clydesdale tractor unit for Road Services (Caledonian). Behind is a rear engined 'Viking' bus which was one of a large fleet of 50 delivered that year to Alexander (Northern), all with 40 seat Alexander bodies. On the Leyland stand is a second generation 'Beaver' truck and an 'Atlantean' for Edinburgh Corporation.

ACKNOWLEDGMENTS.
Grateful thanks to the following friends for their assistance: G. Brackenridge; J. Cairns; P.J. Davies; T. Holdsworth; B. Lambie and Biggar Museum Trust; I. Maclean; T. McAulay; K. McKay; W.G. Steele; I. Taylor; J. Thomson.

BACK COVER.
The Albion 'Lowlander' was known thus only in Scotland. Across the border it was the Leyland 'Lowlander' and indeed it was to all intents and purposes simply a Leyland with Albion badges as all 270 production models were merely assembled at Scotstoun using Leyland parts. The four prototype chassis, however, were manufactured by Albion and seen here towards the end of its life in 1975 is the original 'Lowlander' LR 1 model. It was built in 1961 with an Alexander 72 seat body and appeared that year at the Scottish Motor Show prior to serving as a demonstrator when it visited several operators throughout Britain. In 1962 TCS 151 entered service with Western S.M.T. but was sold in 1966 with several others to fellow Scottish Bus Group member Highland Omnibuses of Inverness where it was photographed with the Castle as a backdrop on a local service to Dell Road. The final Lowlander was built in 1967 and supplied to South Notts of Gotham.